Problem

For I.T. Departments

Darren O'Toole

ISBN: 978-1512113617

First Edition

Copyright © 2015 Darren O'Toole

All rights reserved. No part of this publication may be reproduced, stored in a retrieval system, or transmitted, in any form or by any means, electronic, mechanical, photocopying, recording, or otherwise, without the prior written permission of the author.

A Note from the Author

"Houston, we have a problem!"

That famous phrase from the Apollo 13 mission reminds us just how severe a situation can be when something goes wrong.

Perhaps better terminology, at least according to ITIL, would have been, "Houston, we have an incident!" When the explosion happened aboard the spacecraft it was an unexpected event, or incident, but what followed, both from ground control and from the astronauts, was classic Problem Management at its finest. What went wrong, what was the root cause and what can we do to prevent it from ever happening again?

In this book we look at what Problem Management is all about, why do we need it, how do we get to root cause, reduce incidents, and ultimately, improve our I.T. environment.

While the information in this book is based on ITIL's Service Management best practices, we take it a step further with real world knowledge and first-hand experience.

Best Regards,

Darren O'Toole

Table of Contents

Chapter 1 ITIL Best Practices - Quick Review 1
Chapter 2 Problem Management - Process Overview 6
Chapter 3 Problem Prioritization Scorecard 12
Chapter 4 Roles and Relationships 18
Chapter 5 Root Cause Analysis Techniques 22
Chapter 6 Incident and Problem Reviews 29
Chapter 7 Testing Your Root Cause Theory 33
Chapter 8 Showing Value with Metrics 39
Chapter 9 Training, Testing and Deployment 44
Conclusion and Thanks 48

Chapter 1 ITIL Best Practices - Quick Review

Effective Problem Management is one of the critical keys to success in any I.T. department. Without it, systems continue to break, productivity goes down and the reputation of the I.T. team suffers. The good news is that Problem Management is not difficult, it's not black magic, or smoke and mirrors that only the most advanced engineers can interpret. It is all about taking time to look at what is causing incidents, developing solutions to resolve these underlying problems and carefully implementing the solution by following a change control process.

By following best practice recommendations from ITIL's Problem Management process we can avoid reinventing the wheel and can quickly develop our own in-house Problem Management program.

First, let's take a minute to do a quick review of what ITIL is all about. ITIL, or Information Technology Infrastructure Library, is a framework of I.T. best practices developed in the late 1980's by the

British Government. At the time there was a lack of quality in the I.T. services being provided and the government felt that a set of best practices would help improve efficiencies while driving down costs. As such, they developed standardized processes across a comprehensive range of I.T. services.

The early versions of ITIL, and Version 2 in particular, centered around nine books of best practices. However, during the 2007 revision for Version 3, this was narrowed down to five books forming the ITIL V3 Service Lifecycle as follows:

ITIL's Five Current Publications

1. Service Strategy

2. Service Design

3. Service Transition

4. Service Operation

5. Continual Service Improvement

In 2011 industry feedback and minor corrections were incorporated into an updated version, but no new concepts were introduced. As such, you may hear of ITIL V3, or ITIL 2011. Both are centered around these five books, or core areas of knowledge.

These five books are mapped to ITIL's Service Lifecycle, from understanding customer needs and requirements, through design, implementation and ultimately continual service improvement.

So why choose to follow ITIL? The easy answer is that I.T. departments are always more effective when they follow consistent, repeatable processes. Ad-hoc, or "random I.T." is never efficient and wastes valuable resources constantly reinventing the wheel. While there are many different I.T. best practice frameworks, like the Microsoft

Operations Framework (MOF) for example, ITIL does a good job of bringing everything together in a comprehensive package. Take some time to understand it and make use of some or all of its methodologies in your organization.

In this book we'll expand on one small piece of ITIL, which is Problem Management. This process can be found in their Service Operations book.

Perhaps the one drawback with ITIL is that it is very high level and does not go into detail on how exactly to implement their recommendations. Much of that is left up to trial and error, learning on the fly, or by engaging expensive consultants. By implementing the recommendations here in this book you can save time, money and effort as you roll out your own Problem Management program.

Let's start by defining three ITIL processes that are very closely tied together; Problem Management, Incident Management and Change Management.

Problem Management — officially, ITIL defines a "problem" as the unknown cause of one or more incidents. The focus of Problem Management then is to find the source, or root cause of an incident. The hope is that by getting to the root cause preventive measures can be taken to reduce or eliminate future incidents and their associated impact. Problem Management tends to be reactive when responding to recurring incidents and proactive when part of a continual service improvement effort. Because Problem Management actually reduces incidents, it should be considered one of the most important and value driven processes that directly impacts the bottom line.

Incident Management — an incident is an unexpected event that may, or may not, be affecting an I.T. service. For example, with a redundant environment the incident may not yet be impacting a service, but the agreed to Service Levels are not being met, so this is still an incident. The intent of Incident Management is to resolve the outage as quickly as possible, including using temporary workarounds. Therefore, Incident Management is very reactionary. For a deeper dive into this topic please see my book entitled "Incident Management for I.T. Departments" available on Amazon and Kindle.

Change Management — changes to an environment are either reactive, as in to help resolve an incident, or proactive as in to help reduce problems. The intent of Change Management is to ensure these changes are implemented with standardized methods and procedures. These help minimize possible resulting incidents and potential impact as a direct result of the change. As part of each Request for Change (RFC) a communications plan, a backout plan and a resource plan need to be developed. The RFC also needs to be discussed with the Change Advisory Board (CAB). Each of these steps helps to ensure the change will be successfully implemented and not have a negative impact on the environment.

Problem, Incident and Change Management are three good examples of processes that can lead to a much more efficient and effective I.T. Environment.

Let's look at a real world example to see how effective processes can lead to very high service levels. Recently, I was on a 12 hour flight from Los Angeles to Tokyo. The plane arrived in Tokyo within two minutes of the stated arrival time. Given the changes in weather, aircraft performance, airport flight traffic etc. how could the airline be so precise on a flight that long? Simple, they used well tested processes to accommodate for any variations in the environment and were able to adjust accordingly, meeting my expected service level of arriving on time.

Within I.T. we can also achieve high service levels by following well tested processes, like Problem Management, Incident Management and Change Management. Over time, as we get better at Problem Management we should see the number of incidents start to drop, resulting in a better overall I.T. experience for our user community.

Basing our Problem Management program on ITIL best practices helps ensure we are using a consistent, proven methodology. In the next chapter we will examine the Problem Management process in detail.

Chapter 2 Problem Management - Process Overview

So why should we even deploy a Problem Management program at all? After all, incidents will eventually get resolved and production will be restored. Is there more to it than that?!

Indeed there is! I would be willing to go out on a limb and suggest that Problem Management is one of the most valuable processes within I.T. Think of it this way, if an incident gets resolved, but no steps are taken to find out the root cause, nothing will be done to prevent the incident from happening again. The long term effect then becomes a very unstable and unreliable environment. Not good for any business, or I.T.'s reputation.

There are many additional benefits to implementing a Problem Management program including the following:

- Preventing interruptions to I.T. services
- Meeting Service Level Agreements (SLA's)
- Faster resolution of incidents
- Service availability and quality improvements

- Cost reductions due to system stability
- Staff efficiency and productivity increases
- Increases in overall customer satisfaction

As all of these are desired outcomes for any organization, it makes good business sense then to proceed with developing the Problem Management program. Therefore, let's review the Problem Management process in detail.

Again, Problem Management's focus is all about preventing interruptions to I.T. services, removing recurring interruptions or minimizing the impact of interruptions that can't be prevented. Problem Management includes all activities associated with getting to root cause and deploying the resulting resolutions.

Examples of preventing an interruption, or incident, include patching a software bug, or replacing a defective piece of hardware. To help minimize the impact of a problem regular reboots could be set up to refresh a server's memory leak. While the problem still remains, the reboot ensures the system doesn't crash unexpectedly, thereby minimizing impact.

ITIL's process flow for Problem Management is as follows:

Detection, Logging, Categorization, Prioritization, Investigation, Workarounds, Known Error Record, Problem Resolution, Closure, and Major Problem Review.

Let's look at each in detail…

Detection:

There are several ways a problem can be detected. For example, the Service Desk may notice that they are getting repeat calls about a particular issue. A vendor may issue an alert stating that their software needs to be patched due to a bug. An incident may have occurred where there root cause is not known. Or, through ongoing proactive problem management there may be a fix now available to a known problem that needs to be implemented.

Logging:

Once a problem has been identified all relevant details need to be logged. Hopefully, this can be accomplished with an existing Service Desk ticketing system. Most of the newer Service Desk systems have an option to create a Problem ticket and link it to the associated Incident Records. By linking the tickets you can start to see trends and better identify the relationship between an incident and a known problem.

Categorization:

This field is used to identify trends and help with metrics reporting. Sample multi-level categories could include Hardware – Server – Disks, or Software – Operating System – Windows.

Prioritization:

Prioritization deals with objectively assigning the correct priority to a problem. This priority then drives the appropriate response times, resources and service levels that should be assigned to this level of problem. This is an important step in the Problem Management process and will be discussed in detail in Chapter 3.

Investigation and Root Cause:

The investigation phase is where the real value of Problem Management arises. In later chapters we will cover several different techniques to determine root cause and uncover the real underlying cause of an incident. This includes techniques like The Five Why's, Ishikawa diagrams, and Pareto charts.

Workarounds:

On occasion a temporary workaround may be found for an incident. While this is good news as it restores service more quickly, the Problem Management process must continue to find the root cause and develop a permanent solution.

Imagine that a server has blue screened. The workaround would be to reboot the system, but that doesn't reveal the cause of the problem. A more permanent solution would be to investigate any crash dump files and work with the vendor to find and implement a bug fix.

Known Error Record:

The Known Error Record (KER) is an entry into the Known Error Database (KEDB) that contains details about the problem diagnosis and any workarounds. This is helpful information when another incident occurs as it should lead to quicker resolution of service. Many Service Desk ticketing systems today have a built in KEDB, or at least some type of knowledge base where this information can be stored and referenced.

Problem Resolution:

After a thorough investigation a resolution will eventually be determined. This may require changes to the environment. If so, the appropriate Request for Change (RFC) must be submitted and approved by the Change Advisory Board (CAB). Once approved, the permanent resolution will then be implemented.

It should also be noted that not all resolutions will be implemented. There could be a recommended resolution that is just too expensive to justify, or a vendor may not have a resolution until a future release. In those cases, the Problem Record should be put into a hold state so no further investigation is conducted. The Known Error Record should be updated to reflect any temporary workarounds until the permanent solution is adopted.

Closure:

Once a problem has been fully addressed, and all resolutions implemented, it is safe to go ahead and close the Problem Record. The Known Error Record should also be updated to reflect the permanent resolution has replaced any workarounds.

Major Problem Review:

The Major Problem Review is a deep dive into an incident or problem that has had significant impact on the business. It is recommend to conduct this for anything that scores a Priority 1 on the Priority Scorecard. We'll discuss the Major Problem review in detail later in the book as it is a very important topic.

ITIL's Problem Management Process Flow diagram follows on the next page…

Problem Management for I.T. Departments

ITIL's Problem Management Process Flow

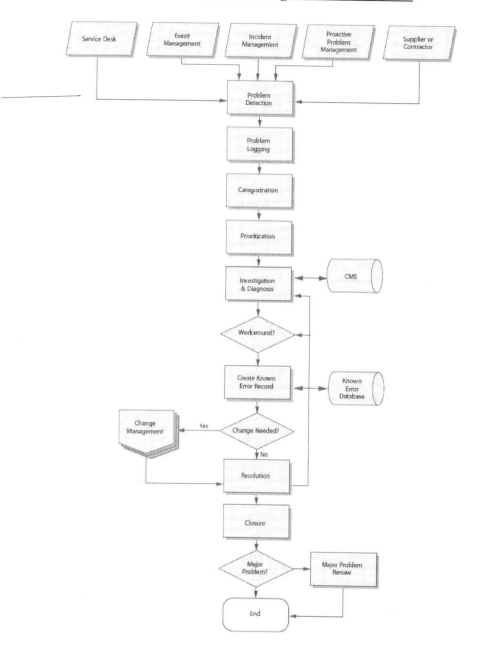

Chapter 3
Problem Prioritization Scorecard

Like most I.T. departments, I am sure yours is very busy. Resources are constrained and budgets are limited. Therefore, it is critical to properly allocate valuable resources so they are focused on the tasks that bring in the most value, or reduce the most pain.

As a Problem Manager, it is very likely that you will find yourself working on multiple problems at the same time. Likewise, some will have a major impact on the company, while others are somewhat benign. Your task is to determine which ones need your highest attention and which ones are less urgent.

The correct way to do this is to prioritize problems objectively so that the right focus can be placed on a problem based on its priority. For example, Priority 1 problems may need to be worked 24x7, while Priority 3 problems could be worked during normal business hours.

ITIL suggests using the following Urgency vs. Impact chart to determine the priority:

Impact vs. Urgency Chart

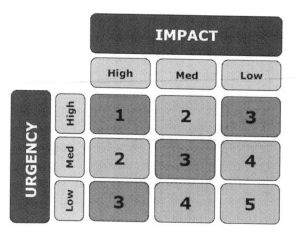

I would like to recommend taking a slightly different approach and using a Priority Scorecard. This same approach can also be used for your Incident Management process. Using ITIL's chart leaves too much to interpretation and is very subjective. For example, if the CEO's email account is down, how does that score on the ITIL chart?

A better real-world approach is to score each problem based on a series of questions that are relevant to your organization. Each question has a point value associated with it. These are then totaled to give you a priority score for the problem.

Take a look at the sample Problem Priority Scorecard on the following page...

Sample Problem Priority Scorecard

PROBLEM PRIORITY SCORECARD		
For This Problem:	Points:	Points Value:
Is this a recurring problem or incident?		If YES add 10 points
What percentage of employees are impacted?		25% to 75% add 10, > 75% add 20
Is this a compliance issue?		If YES add 10 points
Has this been escalated to the Executive level?		If YES add 10 points
Does this problem impact revenue?		If YES add 20 points
Is this a security threat?		If YES add 15 points
Total Points:		

Results:
Priority 1 "Critical" = 50 Points or More
Priority 2 "High" = 25 to 49 Points
Priority 3 "Medium" = If Under 25 Points

In it you can see sample questions that would be specific to your company. Based on these questions, and associated points, which you add to your scorecard, you come up with an overall score. This score then tells you the priority of your incident or problem in a very objective way.

Below are sample questions you may want to include in your own Priority Scorecard:

Sample Priority Scorecard Questions

- Is more than one location impacted?
- What percentage of employees are impacted?
- Is this impacting employees currently on shift?
- To what level of Executive has this issue been escalated?
- Is there a redundant working system carrying the load?
- Does this stop the ability to ship products?
- Is this problem affecting the ability to generate revenue?
- Does this affect the safety and well-being of customers?
- Will this problem lead to a much larger issue if not resolved?

- Will troubleshooting experts be available if I delay resolution?
- Are there financial penalties for this system being down?
- Is this a security threat?
- How much pain is this issue causing the company?
- Does this problem cause us to be out of compliance?
- Are we incurring extra cost while this outage is happening?
- Is this a top tier system that we all agree is always a Priority 1?

One additional consideration in the prioritization phase for a problem versus an incident is the frequency. How often an incident happens, or how many times a particular problem has caused an incident should also be noted in the priority score.

Using these techniques it should be relatively easy for anyone in your organization to determine the correct priority for an incident or problem. The benefit is that everyone is then on the same page and should all be in agreement about how to allocate resources for each issue. It can also help you to justify budget funding for resources. If you find that you are getting an excessive quantity of Priority 1 problems, you should be able to make the business case for more resources to help resolve these.

I would like to suggest one other way to use the Priority Scorecard that helps overcome some Service Desk ticketing system limitations. Many ticketing systems that have a Problem Management module will be based on ITIL. As such, they don't allow you to customize the Impact/Urgency fields within the application and won't allow you to use a Priority Score based solution. However, there is an easy fix to this. Just break down your Priority Score questions into Impact related questions and Urgency related questions. You then use the score of each category to determine whether Impact or Urgency is high, medium or low.

Let's look at an example. Assume "Number of Employees Impacted" is an impact question. We can say that whenever 75% or more of employees are impacted, then this counts as a high impact score. If 74% to 25% are impacted this rates as a medium impact score and if less than 25% are impacted this then rates as a low impact score.

By assigning points to each question we can then group the total impact or urgency question scores together and rate that total score as high, medium or low. The point being that it's critical to keep problem and incident prioritization as objective as possible. If priorities are getting rated different ways by different people you will end up with a very inconsistent process and significant frustration.

Now that you have determined the correct priority for a problem it is necessary to define the correct response, or Service Level Agreements (SLA's), associated with that priority. As mentioned earlier, a Priority 1 might warrant working 24x7 to find a resolution, while a Priority 3 would be worked during business hours.

Cost is another big consideration when responding to high priority problems. If it is a Priority 1 and causing ongoing outages with major impact, you could justify spending extra funds to resolve the issue. A Priority 3 problem may have minimal impact and wouldn't warrant extra expense in the resolution.

A good approach would be to publish all of your SLA's for each priority. This way there is a clear understanding, and expectations are set, on how you will respond once a problem has been determined.

<u>The following SLA's should be clearly stated</u>

- Expected Problem Management response time after detection
- Major problem criteria and expected timeframe for reviews
- Expected timeframe needed to get to root cause
- Anticipated work schedule for each level of priority

- Status report schedules
- Action item response times for assigned tasks
- Anticipated response times from vendors
- Typical testing schedules to help find root cause
- Change Management / Release Management deadlines
- Escalation steps and timeframe for ongoing problems
- Staffing commitments for each priority level

By defining the service levels within your Problem Management process you have carefully managed expectations. You have also created a detailed guideline of what will be done, and when it will be done, within your process. As mentioned earlier, having these repeatable processes will help you be more efficient with your resources.

With these in hand you will also be ready to report on metrics associated with Problem Management. You can then trend performance over time and hopefully show significant improvement in your response and resolution time, plus a correlating reduction in incidents and better overall uptime. We'll look at metrics in detail in chapter 8.

Chapter 4
Roles and Relationships

Now that you've started to develop your Problem Management program, let's take a look at what roles are needed and how typical interactions are played out. We'll also cover responsibilities and suggestions for working across teams.

The first key role in the Problem Management program is the **Problem Manager**. This is the go to person for all things related to Problem Management. In large companies this person will typically lead a team of experts who handle all of the tasks within Problem Management. In mid-sized companies this role may be combined with the Incident Manager role, and in small companies this may be a part time function of the I.T. Manager.

Just a note of caution here when combining the Problem Manager role with other job functions. Think of the intent of the Problem Manager. It is to take a slow, methodical and detailed review of each incident to determine the root cause and clearly identify the problem. On the other hand, the Incident Manager's intent is to get systems up and running as quickly as possible, even if it means implementing a temporary workaround. If these two job roles are combined there is a clear conflict of interest. Think of it this way, an Incident Manager will want to do a quick reboot, while a Problem Manager will want to gather information for a careful analysis. If one person has both roles he or she will have to be careful to collect valuable evidence during an incident, while still working to resolve the impact quickly.

The Problem Manager will be charged with finding root cause and therefore resolving incidents. As such, this can be a very technical role that involves a deep understanding across multiple technologies. It also helps to have a very logical thinker in this role who can take a step by step approach to finding problems.

Another key role in the Problem Management program is the **Incident Manager**. This person is responsible for taking charge when an outage happens and rallying the troops to get systems back up and running as quickly as possible.

While the Incident Management role may be seen as a separate function outside of Problem Management, this person works very closely with the Problem Manager. Both roles are ultimately trying to create a more stable environment for the company so there is always very close cooperation between these roles. These two roles must also be in lock step with information sharing. Both are reliant upon each other for critical data regarding incidents and problems.

Typically, the Incident Manager will share the following information with the Problem Manager; potential workarounds, incident notifications and status updates, and Incident Summary reports. The Problem Manager will typically share the following information with the Incident Manager; confirmed workarounds, status updates, known error information, and close notifications.

Next up is the **I.T. Technician**. The Problem Manager will work very closely with all the technical teams to fully understand the incidents and associated problems. A major component of Problem Management is root cause analysis (RCA), which will involve testing various theories to see if they are the cause of an incident. When conducting this testing the Problem Manager will need to work with technicians to carefully articulate exactly how to test a theory and how to confirm if it is the root cause. The technicians will also be responsible for implementing any recommended changes.

The last key role the Problem Manager will work with is the **Service Desk**. This is the team that will have a lot of the statistics around an incident, like start/stop time, impact, known workarounds, user feedback etc. I suggest building a good relationship with this team as they are an integral part of the process.

One of the key skills of a good Problem Manager is to be able to work across functional teams, even when formal authority may not be in place. The Problem Manager needs to call on resources from multiple teams to help troubleshoot and diagnose problems. Appropriate attendance is also required by the various technical teams, and their management, in Major Problem review meetings. Being able to work effectively with others will go a long way to success.

Given the high visibility of incidents and the desire for stability, senior management will always take a keen interest in the Problem Management program. They want to ensure that continuous improvements are being made and that I.T. has a very good understanding of what is causing the incidents. As such, the Problem Manager needs to be comfortable working with all levels of the organizational chart.

An easy way to get buy in for the Problem Management process, and therefore, good participation across teams, is to be sure everyone understands the value proposition. Effective Problem Management is really the driving force behind increasing stability in the I.T. environment. It is the Problem Manager's task to not only help share this message, but to train and educate others in what Problem Management is all about and why it is valuable. A great way to do this is with lunch and learn sessions. I suggest hosting small group lunches with various members of the overall I.T. department. Put together a few slides on what the process is, how it impacts everyone and why it's valuable. You will be surprised at how successful these sessions can be in getting people on board with the program.

Another great way to get the word out is to present a high level overview in each team's staff meetings. This allows you to tailor your message to an individual department while taking time for questions.

As you can see, not only does the Problem Manager work closely with several other key roles, but he or she has the obligation to reach out to others and help ensure they are on board with the program. By following these few basic steps your program will be on its way to success in no time!

Chapter 5 Root Cause Analysis Techniques

Now that your Problem Management process is starting to take shape let's look at the real key to success in reducing incidents, Root Cause Analysis or RCA.

A good RCA seeks to definitively answer the question of what exactly caused an incident. What systems failed, what went wrong with a process, or what human errors were made that resulted in impact to the user community? Once the root cause has been identified steps can then be taken to resolve the issue, and avoid future issues, thereby leading to improved stability.

A true root cause should be like a light switch, when it is on the incident happens, when it is off, the system does not fail. This may sound simple enough, but it is often difficult to get to this level of certainty. The key is to keep investigating and keep digging deeper into the details to validate the suggested theory of why an incident has happened. It is also possible that a problem or incident may have multiple root causes. That is perfectly acceptable. The intent is to identify the causes and rectify them.

Much has been written about various ways to get to root cause and improve the overall quality of an environment. In this book we will look at a select few techniques that work well within I.T. You may be familiar with other methods that work well for you and your team. That is great! The point is to use whatever method works best to correctly identify root cause and to resolve it.

In order to help facilitate comprehensive root cause analysis discussions we should always consider "**CATWOE**"! What is this you ask? CATWOE, a concept developed by David Smyth in 1975, is a mnemonic that helps identify six key elements that should be considered in problem solving. They are:

1. **C**ustomers — who are they, and how does the situation affect them?
2. **A**ctors — who is involved in the situation? Who will be involved in implementing solutions? And what will impact their success?
3. **T**ransformation Process — what processes or systems are affected by the issue?
4. **W**orld View — what is the big picture? And what are the wider impacts of the issue?
5. **O**wner — who owns the process or situation you are investigating? And what role will they play in the solution?
6. **E**nvironmental Constraints — what are the constraints and limitations that will impact the solution and its success?

With these six key pieces of information, how do we know which problems to tackle first? The best way is with a **Pareto Analysis Chart**. A Pareto chart helps us understand the frequency of a problem, indicating which type of problem is having the greatest effect on our environment. There is a theory in the industry that 80% of incidents can be resolved by focusing on 20% of the problems. Therefore, we should start by focusing on those 20% of the problems.

In the Pareto chart the types of incidents are displayed on the horizontal axis while the quantity are displayed on the vertical axis. The cumulative relative frequency is then superimposed over this bar graph. Because the types of incidents are displayed in order of frequency the graph quickly reveals which issues are having the most impact and where attention should be focused. In the example below we can see that storage, firewall rules and LAN connections make up 80% of our incidents. This is where our focus should be.

Pareto Analysis Chart

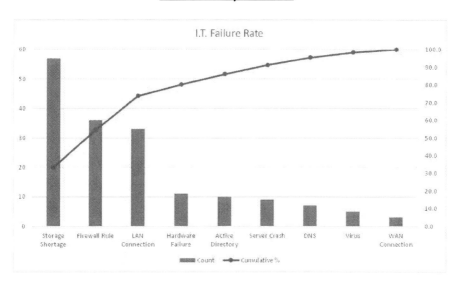

Now that we know what problems to focus on let's look at our first RCA technique, the **Ishikawa**, or **Fishbone** cause and effect diagram. This diagram is very useful in RCA meetings to brainstorm all the possible causes of a problem.

The Problem Manager creates the head of the fish, which is the problem being studied, then draws a line representing the backbone of the fish. The team then identifies several possible causes that may be contributing to the problem and these are drawn as bones of the fish. The team then brainstorms around each of these causes listing additional, related topics of discussion. The conversation continues to break down each cause until the root cause has been identified. This theory can then be tested in the lab to confirm it is correct.

<u>Fishbone Diagram</u>

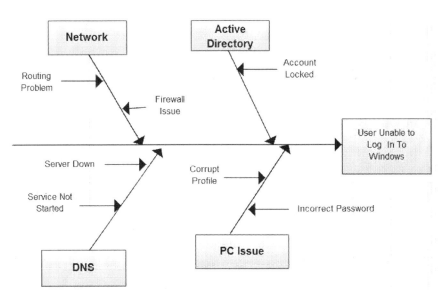

A favorite RCA technique of mine is the **5 Whys**. This involves repeatedly asking the question why for each answer received. While this may bring back memories of your childhood, always asking your parents why, it is a good technique to keep pushing for an answer until you finally get to root cause. Let's look at a humorous example:

The Kingdom has been lost!
  Why?

The Kingdom was lost because the battle was lost.
 Why?
The battle was lost because the Knight was lost.
 Why?
The Knight was lost because the horse was lost.
 Why?
The horse was lost because its shoe was lost.
 Why?
Its shoe was lost because it was missing a nail.

Therefore, the root cause of losing the Kingdom was a simple missing nail in a horse's shoe! Upon first glance, it might be assumed that the Kingdom was lost because the battle was lost. If all remediation effort was focused here at this level, it may not have been effective, or could have proved too costly. By digging deeper with the 5 Whys technique we can see that a much simpler, and more cost effective solution exists.

The benefit of using the 5 Whys technique is that it is very simple and easy to use. It can also be used in combination with other techniques like the Fishbone diagram to dig into potential root causes. I'm always surprised at how effective this technique is in real world problem solving. Just keep asking why and sooner or later you will start to surface additional details that more clearly point to a root cause that you can take action on. You will also find that as you go down each level your solution becomes much more specific and refined. This usually leads to a more accurate fix which typically is easier to implement.

As a general rule of thumb asking why five times will usually be sufficient to getting to a root cause. In some cases you may only need to ask three or four times, but always push for enough detail to make sure that you are focusing on the true root cause.

Let's take one more look at a real world example:

Users cannot login
  Why?
Users cannot log in because the Active Directory server is down.
  Why?
The Active Directory server is down because it ran out of storage.
  Why?
It ran out of storage because the disk on the SAN filled up.
  Why?
The disk on the SAN filled up because no one was monitoring it.
  Why?
No one was monitoring it because the Admin is on vacation.

So we've now found our root cause, the Storage Admin being on vacation. We can now act on this and ensure that a backup Storage Admin is trained and available during any absences.

In some cases there may be multiple problems, or branches of an issue that you need to investigate. In this case, use a branched 5 Whys diagram like the one below. The technique is the same, but you are following multiple paths to multiple root causes.

5 Whys with multiple branches

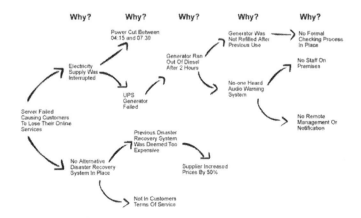

Other techniques you may want to consider as part of your root cause analysis includes Chronological Analysis, Pain Value Analysis, Is-Is Not Analysis, Relations Diagram, Kepner Tregoe Problem Analysis, and just simple brainstorming. As you can see, there are many different ways to conduct a root cause analysis. Try these techniques in your organization and see what works best for you and your team.

Chapter 6
Incident and Problem Reviews

ITIL mentions conducting a **Major Problem Review (MPR)** after solving each "major problem" but doesn't go into detail about how to conduct this meeting. As such, I will explain two different types of meetings that I have used as part of this process.

One of the ways to quickly get to root cause directly after an incident is to host an **Incident Review** meeting. Typically, this would be done for all Priority 1 incidents. The meeting is usually held the next business day after an incident has been resolved, giving people enough time to gather notes and prepare responses. The purpose is to assemble everyone involved, including technical staff and management, to talk through what happened, what was done correctly, what things were done incorrectly, what was the resolution, how good was the incident response, and what were the lessons learned.

As part of your standard templates you should develop a form that everyone must be prepared to help fill out in this meeting. The template should include all of the details regarding the incident including timeframes, impact, who was involved, what was changed, what items still need to be resolved, who owns action items etc.

During the heat of battle, while a system is down, people will be fully engaged in finding a resolution. It makes sense to allow them to focus on getting the system back up and running quickly, but once the dust settles, the Incident Review meeting will give everyone a chance to discuss what happened in detail.

I've found this meeting to be very informative and valuable in determining root cause. It can be surprising how often half the people think one thing was the cause while the other half think it was something else, even though everyone was working on the same incident. By getting everyone into a room, or on a conference call, all the details can be laid out and a consensus reached on what really happened.

Typically, this meeting is where the Problem Manager and Incident Manager work together to start developing action items for the technical teams. For example, a server may have been rebooted, but still needs to have patches applied, or network traffic may have been temporarily routed through a secondary connection due to a fiber cut. Both situations will require follow-up action items to be completed before the incident can be closed.

With the information from this meeting in hand, the Problem Manager can then begin to develop an action plan on how best to prevent this type of incident from happening again. For example, if it was a software patch, this could be a problem on many other servers. The Problem Manager will then assign a task to the Server team to patch all relevant servers. If it was a fiber cut the Problem Manager may set up a meeting with the vendor to see how traffic is being routed and explore alternate paths.

If root cause can't be found for a particular incident by the time this meeting happens, the Problem Manager will note this and prepare a more thorough investigation, with the possibility of a follow up meeting, especially if action items have been assigned. If the incident is similar to other incidents, this could be a definite sign of a major problem. All of this is valuable information to gather as part of the Problem Management process.

Another benefit of this meeting is the overall Problem and Incident Management processes can be evaluated and refined. What other information do these teams need that wasn't available this time around? How could information be shared more effectively? Was information about similar previous incidents readily available in the KEDB? Any time the team is discussing problems and incidents it should be used as an opportunity to improve the overall process. This is fundamental to ITIL's Continual Service Improvement methodology.

The other meeting that is related to ITIL's Major Problem Review is what I call the **Monthly Priority 1 Review** meeting. This meeting occurs once a month and is a deep dive into all high priority incidents and problems. The meeting should be attended by all key players within the I.T. department, including Management, I.T. Architects and Engineers. During the meeting, which is hosted by the Problem Manager, each Priority 1 incident or problem is discussed in detail. This includes a synopsis of what happened, what action items were taken to resolve the issue, what follow-up action items were taken to prevent future occurrences of this issue, and any outstanding action items or issues.

The intent of this meeting is to allow others to dialogue about how an incident or problem was handled. It is an open forum for honest feedback and technical accuracy. Often, more senior engineers will suggest a different way of handling an issue, or management will give guidance on how an action item should be prioritized differently. The meeting usually ends up being very lively with a good interactive dialogue.

The most important aspect of the Monthly Priority 1 Review meeting is that an incident or problem can't be formally closed out until everyone is in agreement and comfortable that all action items are complete. If not, the issue stays open and gets discussed again in the following month's meeting. This ensures there is always follow-up to any action items and issues don't get forgotten about.

I would also suggest inviting Senior Management from other affected departments to this meeting. It shows that issues are being discussed and action items are being addressed. Both help instill a sense of thoroughness by I.T.

Chapter 7 Testing Your Root Cause Theory

All of your analysis, data collection, speculation, and theories are all good stuff, but how do you actually confirm that you have found the true root cause of an incident or problem? Remember earlier when we said that root cause is like a light switch that can be turned on and off? Now is the time to validate that you can really do that. Your next step is to determine what happened, what was impacted, when and where did it happen, how was it detected, how did it happen, and what steps can be taken to stop it from happening again.

Here is the difficult part! You need a test environment where you can make changes and see what happens. Unfortunately, this is not always available so let's look at possible scenarios that will help.

I am a big proponent of building a development, testing, staging, and production environment for all of a company's critical systems. These include anything that you really need to run your business, for example, systems that generate revenue, or meet compliance requirements would usually fall into this category. Think of your disaster recovery plan and your Recovery Time Objective (RTO). The systems with a very short RTO are usually very important to the business. As such, they should be built with sufficient redundancy that testing can be done in a non-production environment.

Whenever you are testing root cause theories it should always be done on non-production systems. There is a high likelihood that something will crash, or need to be restarted. It makes sense to keep these outages from impacting production and customers.

So let's assume it's not a perfect world and you don't have the luxury of a non-production system available? What then?

First, I would suggest setting up recurring **Maintenance Windows**. A maintenance window is a defined period of time during which systems may be down or services may be interrupted. Typically, this would usually occur once or twice a month on a weekend. By publishing this ahead of time as a Service Level Agreement with the business, you then have agreement to take down production systems for maintenance. This can be a good opportunity to test and validate your root cause theories in a production environment.

Another great solution for testing your root cause theories are cloud based environments. Microsoft Azure and Amazon AWS are two environments that will allow you to set up systems on an as needed basis and only pay by the hour. This can be a perfect opportunity to build out a temporary replica of your production environment with minimal cost. In this day and age I would recommend that cloud services be an integral part of all I.T. environments. Having the flexibility and elasticity to quickly create compute environments just makes good business sense.

Other solutions include building an I.T. lab, perhaps from outdated equipment. Even though hardware may be end of life and off the accounting books, it may still have value in a lab. Over time, you may find that you can build a very comprehensive lab, including network and storage systems, just from older hardware. In the event of a major disaster, this may even become the starting point of your recovery environment.

Lastly, don't be shy about asking your vendors for assistance. They will often have a test lab, or demo equipment, that can be very helpful in evaluating root cause testing. They may even go so far as to provide you with hands on technical expertise to help with testing. You probably spend a lot of money with vendors so definitely utilize them to the fullest extent.

Now that you have your equipment and environment in place it's time to actually test your theories. The old adage, try, try again is the key theme with root cause testing. Set up your environment, carefully try a solution, if it doesn't work, make a small change and try again. Best practice is to only make one change at a time so that you can validate it is the true resolution to the problem.

When conducting testing I suggest having the Engineer most familiar with the environment present. I would also suggest building your Problem Management team with people that are very analytical problem solvers. Be sure to have one or two of these people present too. You are going to need to come up with many different test scenarios and possible resolutions for every incident so try to surround yourself with people that ask a lot of questions and can come up with good recommended solutions.

Ultimately, root cause testing comes down to trying a possible solution, letting it run for a while, testing against it, then, if it doesn't work, trying another solution. Unfortunately, there are no shortcuts, but having good problem solvers involved will help reduce the number of iterations this process takes.

As you work through you root cause theory testing you may not be able to get to root cause, or the resolution to root cause may prove to be too expensive, or burdensome to implement. If this is the case then look for a suitable **workaround** or response scenario. This is hopefully, just a temporary solution until a permanent fix can be implemented and is perfectly acceptable.

Workarounds may include things like borrowed hardware or regular reboots during a maintenance window. Anything that will stop incidents and reduce customer impact are helpful while still driving towards a final resolution.

If a workaround is implemented, this should be documented in the **Known Error Database (KEDB)**. The record should include all details about how to implement the workaround and when it should be used. The nature of the incident should also be fully detailed so that the record can easily be found at a later date when a similar incident happens. During an outage, one of the first steps an Incident Manager will do is check the KEDB for anything that looks similar. If there is a record of similar activity the workarounds can quickly be implemented, thereby reducing Mean Time to Resolution (MTTR).

The Problem Manager will also look at the KEDB and any workarounds as part of the problem resolution investigation. Any information that potentially helps point to a root cause should be included in the record.

Now is a good time to discuss Change Management. As part of your theory testing process you will be making many changes to your environment. While most of this should be done in a non-production environment, there is some debate amongst ITIL proponents as to whether this warrants a Request for Change (RFC).

If we look at the intent of Change Management, which is to carefully implement well planned changes, it might make some sense to require an RFC, even for non-production environments. Here's where it gets tricky; one of the biggest complaints about ITIL is how the Change Management process is a major bottleneck, with the Change Advisory Board often only meeting once a week. If we are rapidly trying many different scenarios to get to root cause it may slow down our Problem Management process so much that it's not effective.

Here is some real world experience that might be helpful. Of course, always consider what works best in your own environment. If a change could potentially affect a production environment then I suggest creating the RFC. If there is no chance that the change is going to impact production then I suggest the RFC is not needed.

Let's look at a couple examples. Rebooting a non-production server probably doesn't need an RFC, however, replacing the physical hardware on a non-production server, when it is mounted in the same rack as production servers, does require an RFC. The reason is that there is a good chance that network cables will be disconnected, power unplugged, or something may get accidentally bumped. All of this could cause a production system to go down, therefore going through the Change Management process will ensure everyone is aware and appropriate recovery plans are implemented.

As mentioned earlier, always try to set up an appropriate development, testing, staging, and production environment whenever possible for critical systems. In an ideal world, these environments would even be physically separated in the data center and use infrastructure (storage, networking etc.) that is also isolated. Putting much of this in the cloud can go a long way to easing the complexity of this type of setup.

Once you are confident that your root cause theory testing has revealed the fundamental problem that caused an incident, you are ready to implement a fix.

In some cases this may be as simple as applying a patch, or in other cases, it may mean replacing a very expensive piece of hardware that has consistently proven unreliable. Regardless of the solution, you will always have to go through a cost benefit analysis to ensure your solution is worthwhile. If it is an expensive, or time consuming solution, be sure to use all of your data regarding the impact to the customer to justify your recommendations. In the next chapter we'll look at how metrics can prove invaluable in these cases.

Chapter 8
Showing Value with Metrics

We have learned that fundamentally, as we implement our Problem Management program, the number of incidents we experience will be reduced. As a result of this, the quality of the I.T. services we offer will go up and our committed to service levels can be raised. This also means that over time, resources allocated to Incident Management can be repurposed to Problem Management, continuing the cycle of improvement.

All of these scenarios are a tremendous value to the business and need to be highlighted in meaningful ways to management and our stakeholders. We need to be able to demonstrate metrics showing significant improvements over time as a result of our process. But how do we do that?

First, let's be sure that we fully understand the value of our new Problem Management program. Remember the foundational intent of Problem Management? It is to reduce the number and associated impact of incidents, leading to a higher quality of I.T. service. Now we need to develop key performance indicators, or metrics, that will drive changes in behavior and improve business outcomes.

Sample Metrics that Demonstrate Value

- **Number of Incidents:** record and chart the number of incidents over time. This should trend downwards as the Problem Management process begins to reduce overall incidents.

- **Number of Repeat Incidents:** record how often the same incident is repeated. This should trend down as Problem Management finds solutions to recurring incidents.

- **Number of Priority 1 Incidents:** this metric is very important as Priority 1 incidents usually have major impact. By decreasing these over time with our process, we are having a very positive impact on the business. Likewise, the number of priority 1 reviews in the monthly review meetings should go down.

- **Number of New/Resolved Problems:** like incidents, the number of problems should also trend down with a focused effort on Problem Management. This can also be broken down further into problems that have caused incidents (reactive) and problems that were resolved before an incident occurred (proactive).

- **Mean Time to Resolution:** measure the MTTR of an incident. As the Known Error Database becomes populated with workarounds the MTTR should decrease. Faster response means less impact to the business.

- **First Call Resolution:** this metric measures how often a Service Desk can resolve an issue without having to escalate to more senior engineers. With the KEDB in place the Service Desk will have a very valuable tool to resolve a large percentage of incidents.

- **Number of Workarounds:** as this number increases there are more known workarounds available to fix incidents. Also important is to show the number of workarounds that have been converted into permanent solutions.

- **Top 5 Problems by Month:** be sure to show what problems have caused the most concern, even if they are not resolved. This metric will be a good way to increase dialogue across I.T. and get a larger audience thinking about resolutions. You may also tie in a metric here that shows the previous month's Top 5 problems that have been resolved.

- **Backlog of Open Problems:** track what has not been resolved yet and why. A note of caution here. Metrics that measure things like "time to root cause" may put undue pressure on the team to offer a root cause that may not be accurate. Give them time to dig in to the details and get to the true root cause, it will pay dividends in the long run.

- **Problem and Incident Cost:** this one can be challenging to accurately determine, but if you can show the cost of an incident or problem, it helps drive a sense of urgency for improvement. Think of all the costs involved in an incident: how many people were idle? What support costs had to be paid? Was any hardware or software purchased? Did you lose revenue or customers? Each of these can reinforce the value of a good Problem Management program.

- **Value Stream:** this one is specific to your organization. In what ways has Problem Management reduced costs or increased productivity? Have you been able to ship more product, or generate more revenue, as a result of improved uptime? Show this with a meaningful metric.

- **Customer Satisfaction Rating:** send out regular customer surveys and track how your process improvements are increasing their satisfaction levels.

Be sure to trend all of your metrics over time. The key is to show that things are improving as a result of your efforts. A single metric may not say much, but a trend is very meaningful. Trends will also help you to not only predict future events, but adjust your resources and goals accordingly. If you see that the Service Desk will be handling 90% of incidents in six months, now might be the time to add staff in that area to help with the workload. If workarounds mostly seem to point to patching issues, then you'll want to develop a more thorough patch testing process. Use the information to change behavior.

If your I.T. department doesn't already do a monthly operational review, then I would suggest setting up a separate meeting to share these metrics with leadership. You may also want to show these in your Monthly Priority 1 Review meeting.

Remember that metrics are intended to change behavior so each must be meaningful in some way and have a call to action. As an example, if the number of incidents is trending up, the action item is to investigate why. Perhaps it is a lack of resources, or a new patch has been applied to all servers. Either way, the metric is showing that action needs to be taken soonest to reduce incidents.

In additional to the metrics shown above, there are probably several others that are relevant to your organization. In your metrics meetings with management take note of which ones create the most interesting dialogue and see if you can expand on these to be even more meaningful. I've always found that discussing five or six key metrics is much more productive than a 30 or 40 metric slide deck. Be sure to stay focused on your value proposition as you are wanting to demonstrate that your Problem Management program is creating value for the company.

Chapter 9 Training, Testing and Deployment

We've now seen several key steps to developing your Problem Management program. How do we now take this information and roll it out into a real life process that is bringing value to your organization?

The first step is to share the process with your colleagues and build internal support across all levels of the organization. While in this initial sharing phase keep it high level and focus on the benefits of the program. Be sure to make note of any feedback that can be used to improve the process.

Once you've gathered feedback and have initial support, set up meetings with various members of the I.T. and business leadership teams. In these sessions describe how the program will improve their specific environments and what resources you may need from them. Be sure to have a fully polished business plan ready to present all aspects of your proposal.

With leadership's support, you are now ready to move into the deployment phase. Set goals and timelines for your rollout and be sure to maintain a detailed project plan. Just like any other I.T. project, this effort needs to be managed and measured carefully for success.

For the next step in preparing to roll out your process you will need to put some thought into your overall workflow for both Problem Management and Incident Management. Workflow involves determine how an incident or problem flows through all of your resources and systems. It also sends alerts or updates to the correct people helping ensure SLA's are being met during each step of the process. Getting a good workflow designed will help ensure all issues are properly tracked and resolved.

<u>Typical Problem Workflows</u>

- Steps taken to initiate and handle a problem
- Chronological order these steps should be taken in, including dependencies
- Responsible parties, who does what
- Timescales and thresholds for action item completion
- Escalation procedures, who should be contacted and when
- Evidence preservation activities, especially for security and capacity issues

Many Service Desk ticketing systems are designed around ITIL's best practice recommendations. If so, it is very likely that you will be able to automate many of the workflow steps within your process. Some, like ServiceNow, even have built in Structured Problem Analysis methodologies based on Kepner Tregoe's techniques. Definitely talk with your ticketing system vendor to better understand the capabilities of your environment. In many cases the tools will help automate much of the Problem Management workload.

Next you need to ensure everyone understands their role in Problem Management. To help facilitate this it is important to provide both formal and informal training. For direct participants in the Problem Management process an ITIL Foundations class would be very helpful. Not only does this cover Problem Management, but also the other core ITIL processes that may be very useful in your environment.

Informal training can be covered with lunch and learn sessions and in-house classes. By taking time to share this new process with all of I.T. you will get buy-in and support across the organization. It also helps everyone understand expectations, especially if they are involved in some aspect of the process.

In-house classes should include running various past problems and incidents through your process to see how they play out. Do they score correctly on the Priority Scorecard? How would they look on a Pareto chart? What would the 5 Whys reveal? Did you dig deep enough into them to get to true root cause and come up with a resolution? By answering these questions about real scenarios in your own environment you can test your process and fine tune any needed changes.

With training and testing complete it's time to go live with your new process. Pick a go-live date that allows everyone enough time to prepare. Be sure that all the right resources are lined up and ready for the big day. It may also help build support by advertising the go-live on your intranet web site, or in company town hall meetings.

For the first few weeks that the process is live continue to evaluate it and tweak it accordingly. Set up meetings with your peers to solicit their impression of the process and be sure to incorporate their feedback in any changes.

As you start to gather metrics be sure to share these too. Initially, you may see incidents and problems actually increase, but this is usually because everyone is now carefully tracking things that may have slipped through the cracks in the past. Over time, problems and incidents should definitely trend downwards, uptime should increase, user impact should decrease, and customer satisfaction should increase. If so, congratulations! You have now rolled out a well-planned Problem Management program.

Conclusion and Thanks

Problem Management can be very challenging! You think you've finally found root cause, then yet another incident happens! It can ultimately also be very rewarding. There is a certain satisfaction in finally solving the elusive cause of recurring incidents and improving overall stability in the environment.

By embracing the challenge, getting good people and processes in your program and staying focused on continual service improvement, you will soon be well on your way to implementing a successful Problem Management program!

I would like to personally thank you for taking time to read this book. Information Technology has been a passion of mine for 30 years and has been a very enjoyable career. I hope you find it just as compelling and rewarding.

Best Regards,

Darren O'Toole

Darren_OToole@Advantiga.com

Made in the USA
Lexington, KY
02 January 2016